the PECKING ORDER
IN RELATIONSHIPS

the

PECKING ORDER

IN RELATIONSHIPS

This book will help you define and redefine the status of   your relationships. Know where you are in the social pecking order!

DARRYL O. GRIFFIN, D. Div.

Published by
Darryl O. Griffin Ministries
P.O. Box 1333
Cordova, TN 38088
www.darrylogriffin.com

ISBN: 978-1-7346581-4-9 Paperback
        978-1-7346581-5-6 Digital

Printed in the United States of America

Contents

Foreword

They say that in the world of real estate, the three most important words are *location, location,* and *location*! My truest belief and conviction is that the three most important words are *relationships, relationships,* and *relationships* in today's culture—both church and community! If there's ever been a time to address the ever—importance of relationships masterfully, **now** is the time, and Dr. Griffin is the **person**!

As we move toward this post-pandemic era of our day and time, there is an all-out war against quality and lasting relationships, whether between husband and wife, parent, and child or between best of friends. In fact, there is a vile and abhorrent social and cultural agenda and attack against the traditional core values of foundational, Godly relationships in our world today.

Dr. Darryl O. Griffin has simply nailed it! The Pecking Order in Relationships by Dr. Darryl addresses head-on and open honesty the many challenges and obstacles many of us face today by providing sound wisdom and practical solutions to strengthen our day-to-day relationships. Truth is...his writing is both divinely appointed and anointed for such a time as this—to critically contemplate through and cautiously advise tomorrow's generation on the importance of relationships and their many influences in our lives today.

Dr. Michael A. Stevens, Sr., D. Min.
Charlotte, NC

Adjunct professor at Oral Roberts University, Tulsa, Oklahoma (2019 to Present)

Authored:
"Holy Spirit in the Now!" (Self-Publishing, 2022)
"We Too, Stand: A Call for the African-American Church to Support the Jewish State" (Frontline Publishing, 2013)
"No More Excuses: Creating a Culture in the Church to Reach African-American Men" (Charisma House, 2008)
"Straight Up: The Church's Official Response to the Epidemic of Downlow Living" (Creation House, 2006).

Introduction

Hello, reader. I am excited to have this extraordinary opportunity to share this book with you today. I hope you are ready to go on a relationship journey to see your relationship scale.

Joshua chapter one is not for people who are still wandering or wondering. In the Book of Joshua, God deals with the pecking order in relationships. Therefore, walking people are about to step into their destiny and purpose. There's new leadership in Joshua.

Moses, my servant, is dead. Some of the relationships you once had, ended. Somebody, please declare today, "Moses is dead." That means the former grace of enduring and surviving that relationship is over. Moses had an anointing to help a group of people weather the bleak terrain of a desert. He led them through the wilderness. When Moses got to the end of the wilderness, he died. A new leader named Joshua took over, whose anointing was not to wander. Joshua was a fighter, a warrior, and a possessor of the promises of God. Some people had to exit your life for God to put new people in your life so that you would become a possessor of the promises of God.

Moses was dead. God gave them a certain number of days to weep for Moses, and when the day of mourning was over, God said, "Moses, my servant, is dead. As I was with Moses, so shall I be with you, Joshua." Just because a relationship has ended doesn't mean that God is not with you. It's okay to take time to mourn any relationship that has ended. A clinical psychologist says that the process of dealing with a breakup or ended relationship is comparable to grief. It's the death of a relationship, hopes, and dreams for the future. The person we are losing was a big part of our inner and outer world and therefore has taken up so much of our mental and heart space. But your mourning season has expired for many of you reading this book. Dry your face. Stop crying. It's time to cross over. Listen carefully; I want to pronounce to you today; a benediction on every grieving, weeping, depressed, lonely, frustrated, and tired relationship that God ended. Your season of mourning is over. Tell your girlfriend, your bestie, your cousin, your church member; I cried my last tear yesterday. Today declare it from the rooftop; I cried my last tear yesterday, so you can send those flowers back and return that sympathy card. Stop looking all pitiful and seeing me as a charity case. I got my strength back! I got my fight back! I got my vision back because my season of mourning is over!

I'm forgetting those relationships behind me and reaching to those new relationships before me. I got some "press down" in me. That's how I can move forward past the hurt and the pain because I got some "press down" in me. That's why I can start cultivating these new relationships because I got some press in me. I got some fight in me. I can't worry about past relationships that ended.

If you don't believe I got some press in me, look back at my history and ask those who fought me. Ask the people who said I would never make it. Ask the people who abandoned and didn't prioritize the relationship. I made it without them, and I made it despite them.

In Joshua's chapter two, he sends out a couple of spies and sends them in to spy out the land before he ever takes it. And interestingly, he would send spies out to spy out the land, considering he had been one of Moses's spies. So, he didn't need them to spy out the land because he didn't know what was there; he had already been there.

So why did he send them? Why did a man who had been to Jericho himself now send these spies over to the promised land? You remember Joshua had been there before with the spies. Now he sends these two spies over there and says, "I want you to scope out the land."

Because you cannot lead people into anything that you don't have a vision for, that's number one. Number two, God wants you to be excited about your new relationships so that you can endure the process that brings you into promise. Because there is a process before the promise, and if you don't have at least a vision of the promise, the process will discourage you. But every time discouragement tries to get you to give up on the process, remember the image you have of the promise. Stay connected to the people trying to help you get to your destination. Having the right relationships in your life enables you to get to your destination without it becoming a train wreck. Humans are social beings—and the quality of our relationships affects our mental, emotional, and physical health. Let's begin our relationship journey as we detox and unpack our baggage. The goal of the healing process is to unpack and deal with any baggage from your previous relationship(s) before embracing another. Some people have a hard time understanding why the same problems keep occurring. If you don't address those things head-on in this new season, you will bring the same baggage, issues, and drama in your next relationship.

CHAPTER 1

WARNING SIGNS
OPTION vs. PRIORITY

So, let's begin this relationship journey. How do you know where you are on the social relationship scale? Pecking Order...what is it? **Pecking Order is an informal social system in which some people or groups know they are more or less important than others: (Cambridge Dictionary).** My definition of Pecking Order is the order of importance of people on your social scale.

No one wants to find that they are not a priority in their relationships. It is a hard realization to come to, but too many people tend to ignore the signs that they are not a priority by rationalizing them away. I see people often in the workplace, family, and even in the church trying to cultivate and even label the relationship as number one on their social scale. When the other person is afraid to tell them that you're not number one on their social ranking, you very well may be two or three. Of course, you can rationalize these signs, but when a significant person in your life is presenting you with more than a few signs, it may be time to reassess and redefine the relationship.

Dangers that Lurk in Relationships

• **You make all the concessions in the relationship—if it can be called a relationship.**
• **They're always jealous when other people want to spend time with you, like your spouse, family, or another close friend.**
• **The person makes you feel bad, depressed, or unhappy more than they make you feel happy.**
• **They act secretive and suspicious like they're constantly hiding something.**
• **You feel like they're bored when they're around you.**
• **They never seem to show any interest in your life or the things that you do daily. When you do talk about things, they tend not to remember.**
• **They do not understand important things to you and often forfeit important events for their plans, sometimes canceling at the last minute.**
• **You catch them lying to you about seemingly insignificant things.**
• **You feel taken advantage of by them. This point is vital because intuition is often correct, and when it feels like someone doesn't care, it is because they are not expending the effort to**

show you that they care.
• Your calls, texts, emails, Facebook messages, and so on go unanswered. We all know that almost everyone is attached to their phone today; you know they saw the communication and chose not to respond.
• There are always excuses regarding why they don't have the time to spend with you: if someone wants a relationship with you, they'll find a way. Excuses mean a lack of investment and often a lack of mutual interest.

After reading this list: Are you an option or priority? Let's be honest! Do you know where you are on the social relationship scale?

Everyone makes mistakes in relationships but learning when to let go because of a lack of mutuality is an important life lesson to learn. These signs, especially when more than four or five are present are warning signs that indicate when it might be time to let the relationship go, re-evaluate, or redefine it, even if it's a co-worker, family member, or even a church member. In my many years of Pastoral counseling, I discovered that many people start to go down two different paths in life. They want to make the relationship work out so bad that they ignore all the warning signs that the relationship has moved down the social pecking order scale. Some people are not ready to admit this truth. Even when every hidden fiber within us tells us to let it go or redefine the relationship, we stay and hold on to a relationship that's past its expiration date. Human beings are genetically programmed to desire love. Love is as essential to us as food and water. You can still love people at a distance. **"Relationships are like glass. Sometimes it's better to leave them broken than to hurt yourself trying to put it back together." – Unknown**

You Were Made for RELATIONSHIP

God created us not only as spiritual beings but also as social beings. We were made for RELATIONSHIP. This chapter deals with Relation-SHIP 101.

God said it was not good for us to be alone (Genesis 2:18). So, he gave us relationship.

Relationship is how two or more people regard and behave toward each other. Relationship can be applied to connection either by birth, marriage, or another connection.

Much of what we're to gain, learn, and experience from functional and healthy relationships reflects the kind of connection God wants to have with us. He shows us momentary or partial views of himself through his people in our lives. Isn't that amazing!

Not only that, but you and I can also be a tangible expression of God's love for people through how we interact with, connect with, and care for them through our relationships. What an incredible, even overwhelming reality!

Before we do a deep dive into this chapter, it's only fair to warn you that I'm not an "expert" in relationships. I grew up in a large family with two Christian parents; I've been serving people in ministry for over 30 years and married to the same woman for over 33 years. These are just some of my qualifications to share wise counsel regarding this subject with my readers.

I've heard many people use the label BFF: Best Friend Forever. People used to loosely sign their high school yearbook with this common cultural label.

We usually have more than one "best" friend, so the whole thing doesn't make sense to me. But humor me. Try to think of the first best friend you ever had. Do you remember what the basis of that friendship was?

My first childhood besties were Willie Walker, Kevin Bradley, and Terry Watts; we were the four amigos.

What made them my best friends? We lived in the same hood. We were around the same age, attended the same school, and were bullied by the same bully. My wife would say, "FUNNY!" That's what connected us, the everlasting bond of location, age proximity, experienced bullying together and attendance at the same educational institution. People eventually grow up, attend college, get married, have children, start their career path, and go in different directions. After adulthood, we tend to forget that adult friend-SHIPS take a whole lot of time, commitment, emotional energy, and many hours of work. I don't think I'll ever forget my childhood besties' memories, but life happened. And the many different things in life caused us to drift apart as we got older. I haven't spoken with my childhood besties in over 30 years. So even in my teens, they were at the top of my pecking order scale. If you asked me today, where do they fall in my social pecking order scale, I would honestly have to say at the bottom of my pecking order scale. If they are married, I wouldn't know their spouses. I wouldn't know their children or grandchildren. I can't say I would know their religious beliefs or career paths, likes, or dislikes. People tend to hold on to labels because they make us feel secure. I still love those guys but couldn't honestly say that if I connected with them today, they would all move quickly up my social pecking order scale. People have a specific longing for a best friend or another relatable person—someone who knows our heart and intimate secrets have seen our victories and failures—someone to help us get through life's most brutal storms. Even the shyest and most introverted of us, I think if we're being honest, long for that kind of relationship. For most people, it's a position that only a friend can fill.

I think the desire for a close, trusted, and committed friend is a natural longing that God wired into us. Now that I'm a lot older, wiser, have more experience, and have studied the true nature of people over the years; I'm very cautious about labeling people as best friend. Sometimes God allows certain people to come into our lives for a season and when that season is over, they leave. Some people are loose with that label. I've noticed adults getting jealous at the sound of someone they're in a relationship with referring to someone else as their best friend. They start feeling insecure, left out, excluded, and alone. When I hear a woman refer to another woman as her best friend, I immediately hear, I'm unavailable. That position has been filled in my life. No other friend will compare to her. I will not move anyone else up in my pecking order. My devotion is to her. All my other friends come second. I mean, it is the word "best" after all.

When many people hear that someone has a best friend, they feel like they will never be considered worthy of a deep connection with this other person because their time, emotions, and commitment are already tied to their best friend. I've seen people use the label best friend as a tool to manipulate the relationship. Because of their insecurities, they can't stand to see the person they're in a relationship with move someone else up on the social pecking order scale. Beware! Sometimes when people use the label "best friend", it's to ward off outside intruders. They feel threatened when their friend has a close friend. When I think about this chapter, I can't recall ever hearing my besties using the label "best friends." It was simply a natural bonding relationship that four boys experienced together.

Please understand the position I've taken. I'm not saying it is wrong to use the label "best friend." There are several godly people in my life that I adore and respect who frequently share this label "best friend." I consider my wife Lenora my best friend, and she considers me her best friend. I do not believe we are trying to communicate any message of unavailability or exclusion. I don't think our motives are to cause any jealousy. Some people use the label "best friend" healthily to build up their friendship. It's a public compliment for someone significant to them. And honestly, it likely does mean that their best friend takes priority in their life. But please know that I've seen many women use this label "best friend" to manipulate the other person's relationships because of their insecurities and selfishness. Some people can't be happy for someone else unless it's with them. So, what makes a genuinely long-lasting "best" friendship? I believe it's a combination of shared interests, shared values, similar senses of humor, chemistry, commitment, loyalty, and kindred spirits if you're fortunate. Why is it that, even from a young age, we long to belong, to relate with someone, to be in the "in" crowd, to be known, to have a best friend or, as one of my cousins would say, be part of "the inner circle?"

The Beginning of Relationship

If we want to see how this whole relationship thing started, we need to go back to the first chapter of the book of the Bible, Genesis.

"Then God said, "Let us make mankind in our image, in our likeness, so that they may rule over the fish in the sea and the birds in the sky, over the livestock and all the wild animals, and over all the creatures that move along the ground. So, God created mankind in his own image, in the image of God he created them." (Genesis 1:26-27 NIV)

Now, if we fast-forward to Genesis chapter two, God tells us it wasn't good for man to be alone, so He made him a helper.

From chapter one, the Bible tells us that we were created to enjoy a relationship with God (Genesis 1) and relationships with each other (Genesis 2). Sadly, it didn't take long for these relationships to get messed up.

Just a few chapters later, Adam and Eve shared a piece of the only fruit in the garden God asked them not to eat, and it's all been downhill from there. Ever since then, we've been trying to get back to the perfect, untainted, ultimately fulfilling relationship with God, and healthy functional relationships with each other. But we are often hindered by the lasting effects of Adam and Eve's choice and the choices we all make today, namely the stubborn selfishness or self-will known as sin.

In my opinion, this is what makes Christianity so unique. The God we worship wants a personal relationship with us! Christianity isn't about a bunch of do's and don'ts, rules, or restrictions; it's about a personal relationship with our Creator and with each other. And only Jesus Christ can enable this to happen, redeeming us and restoring what God originally intended.

In (Genesis 1:27) this verse tells us we are made in His image. We have the privilege of learning something very intimate about God in **Jeremiah 9:24, where the Lord tells us that if a man boasts about anything, it should not be his wisdom, strength, or even his possessions. Instead, it should be his understanding and knowing God.** A few chapters later, He says something fundamental: **"I will give them a heart to know me, that I am the LORD." (Jeremiah 24:7 NIV)**

Since we are made in God's image and He values being known more than anything else, it stands to reason that it is imperative for us as humans also to be known.

We are made for relation-SHIP, which I believe is a gift from God. Something in us makes us want to belong, be known, and be understood. Not only do we want to be known by God, but we have a high need to be known by others here on earth.

CHAPTER 3

Friends for Dummies

Many of us struggle with this concept of friendship. We can probably count on one hand how many true friends we have. Remember the song "Friends" by the American hip-hop group Whodini? If you think about it, Whodini might have been on to something. All of us have experienced the complexity of having friends. It is challenging because many of us have experienced wounds and bitterness from our so-called friends. **"A man who has friends must himself be friendly, But there is a friend who sticks closer than a brother." (Proverbs 18:24 NKJV)**

This chapter aims to explore who doesn't qualify to be your friend. **Proverbs 1:10 says, "My son if sinners entice thee, consent thou not."** King Solomon says we must be careful about our associations because those associations can bring about assimilation, which means you could be in grave danger of evolving into the people you associate with or hang around. That is where the whole idea, "birds of a feather flock together" originates. Assimilation is like a battery. It is a word that has both positive and negative charges. If used correctly, there are many positive possibilities for those who conform willingly. However, if harmful components exist, it can cause a relationship to collide and derail a person's entire life. I've discovered that you evolve into the people you hang around: in your relationships, marriage, ministry, and personal life. At least three to five people around you determine your success, and they are the people you choose. Every benefit you want to receive in a relationship will depend on the type of connection. You cannot benefit from the fruits of prosperity when you are connected to impoverished people. You cannot benefit from wise counsel when connected to foolish advice. You cannot benefit from a loving relationship when connected to an abusive relationship. You cannot benefit from the blessings of God when you are connected to a sinful lifestyle. Many years ago, I preached a message entitled **"Your Connections Affect Your Direction."** Whomever you are connected to will precipitate what will come to you. You must examine who you are connected to in this season because it will determine if God rewards you or if you come under His judgment. Make sure you choose your friends wisely so that you will not carry the weight of suffering on your shoulders. If your life is consumed with confusion, losses, mess, drama, and misfortune due to your CONNECTIONS, then you are suffering unnecessarily. Before continuing this chapter, I want to explain the concept "for dummies." I'm not writing this chapter to be offensive to anyone. When people hear the word dummy, they think of another word. Does stupid come to mind? No, not in this case, "for dummies" means something explained in length for laymen in straightforward terms. Usually, the phrase is used for guidelines and instructions in simple steps so that anyone can follow them easily, even without in-depth knowledge on the subject. Here are some practical kingdom principles about friends for dummies.

Avoid Friendships with these People

Please stay away from **Violent People.**
These are people I'm apprehensive about being around. They throw things, storm off while trying to discuss a matter, and talk with an elevated voice whenever disagreement comes up with no solution to offer. I know from time-to-time people have heated disagreements. My wife and I call these heated disagreements "intense fellowship." But whenever we disagree, we always offer solutions to the problems.

Stay away from **Greedy People.**
Proverbs 1:19 (NKJV) says, "So are the ways of

everyone who is greedy for gain; It takes away the life of its owners." A greedy person's primary goal in life is to get more and more of something they want, and their whole focus is on getting it. Although, we think of money when we think of greed. Still, a person can be greedy for other things like fame, possessions, success, prestige, etc. Even if it's another person's spouse, career, ministry, or status in life. These are people that are in pursuit of things all the time. They always want more.

Manifestations of Greedy People

Something for nothing attitude * It's all about me mindset * Robs other's confidence * Will do anything to get what they want * Manipulate people * Steal from you as if you don't know they are stealing from you * Think they are better than others once they arrive at a certain level

Stay away from **Froward People.** They swerve from one side to the other; they can't make up their mind. The adverb froward is an old-fashioned way to describe someone difficult, hard to deal with, going from one extreme to another. **Proverbs 2:12 says, "To deliver thee from the way of the evil man, from the man that speaketh froward things."** There is no stability in their lives. You can't build a long-lasting friendship with this type of person.

Stay away from **People Who Despise Knowledge. Proverbs 1:29 says, "For that they hated knowledge, and did not choose the fear of the LORD:"** These are people you know who do not want to grow in the word of God. Often, people who don't want to do better don't want you to do better because when you do better, you intimidate them. If you both struggle and remain on the same level or status—as my teenage son, Davien, would say, "they're straight."

Stay away from **Immoral People.**
They will say and do anything. Immoral people don't have a moral compass or Holy Ghost filter. **Proverbs 2:16-19 says, "To deliver thee from the strange woman, even from the stranger which flattereth with her words; Which forsaketh the guide of her youth, and forgetteth the covenant of her God. For her house inclineth unto death, and her path unto the dead. None that go unto her return again, neither takes they hold of the paths of life."** These types of people, in many cases, don't bring value to the relationship. In any case, you must decide whether and what value these people bring to your life and determine what level of involvement or lack thereof is appropriate.

Stay away from **Talebearers.**
These are people that enjoy gossiping about

others. A talebearer is only interested in sharing juicy information about other folks, no matter the negative effects on those people. **Proverbs 10:19 says, "In the multitude of words there wanteth not sin: but he that refraineth his lips is wise."** Here is my translation of this scripture: Make a practice of shutting down conversations in person or on social media that aim to tear down or destroy another person's reputation. There comes a time in your life when you must realize if they gossip about everyone to you, then they are talking about you too. Let the church say, "Amen!"

Stay away from **Liars.**
Proverbs 14:5 says, "A faithful witness will not lie: but a false witness will utter lies." These people make up stuff. Sometimes these people make up lies to make themselves look good. So, what's the truth about lying? What harm does it cause? Lying is poisonous to relationships of all kinds, no matter where you are on the social pecking order scale. The most apparent impact lying has on a relationship is the erosion of trust one person has in the other. It will not be seen right away but happens over some time. Lies and trust cannot easily coexist; eventually, the former will destroy the latter in any relationship.

Stay away from **Angry People.**
Proverbs 15:18 says, "A wrathful man stirreth up strife: but he that is slow to anger appeaseth

strife." These are the people that make you nervous about being around. You don't feel comfortable going to the movies or dinner with them. They are always ready to fight or display some negative energy publicly. You must tiptoe around this type of person which is unhealthy and dysfunctional. Angry exchanges are bound to happen between friends. Ranging from mild to explosive, they are often likely to create cumulative damage over time. They are often preceded by feelings of frustration, hurt, unmet needs, or perceived injustice. Because the person on the other end of angry expressions cannot see those hidden feelings, they too often react defensively to the anger itself. The offense becomes contagious, and the result is a downward spiral with two upset people misunderstanding the underlying reasons for why they are having a dispute.

Stay away from **Lazy People.**
Proverbs 10:5 says, "He that gathereth in summer is a wise son: but he that sleepeth in harvest is a son that causeth shame." Synonyms for laziness are indolence and sloth. Indolence derives from the Latin word indolentia, "without pain" or "without taking the trouble." These people, without any ambitions, only sit around trifling and have no regard for deadlines or schedules. They want to chill without investing anything into the relationship. Relationships are hard work. However, I've realized that these

kinds of friendships are so rare these days. The concept of friendship itself has changed into something fickle and surface based. I know that I have a certain number of friends on my personal Facebook page but barely can any of those people be classified as true friends. This laziness is a spirit, and it is contagious. A person is lazy in the relationship if they can carry out some activity that they ought to carry out but is disinclined to do so because of the minimal effort involved.

Stay away from **Drunkards.**
We all know people who drink, but this type of person loses control every time they take a drink. Alcohol numbs the senses and can ruin your relationship. Drinking excessively or too often can have consequences, one of which is damaged relationships. If you're reading this part, I'm not here to pass judgment on anyone nor to debate anyone's religious conviction. But in my ministry experience, no one wants to lose the love and trust of someone they care about over something preventable. We will always be in a dysfunctional relationship with this person because we never know who will show up. These people jeopardize us because we don't know what they will do or say.

Stay away from **Fools.**
Psalm 14:1 says, "The fool hath said in his heart, There is no God. They are corrupt, they have

done abominable works, there is none that doeth good." Having foolish friends will cause you to REAP their troubles, inherit their losses, adopt their struggles, and share their hardships. Fools are just fools. The friends of fools will suffer because they are CONNECTED to foolishness. Please know that you do not have to do anything wrong to suffer unnecessarily; you only must connect with the wrong person. FOOLISH PEOPLE ARE POISON TO YOUR SUCCESS! Every benefit you want to receive will depend on the type of connection you have.

This exhaustive list names just about everyone we know for some of us. I'm not suggesting that you look for perfect friends, nor do you eliminate everyone you know from your social circle, but it is dangerous to befriend someone without examining their character first. I've seen this happen too many times. Who you invite into your social circle to be a friend will alter everything in your life? They will either position you to succeed or fail, obey God, or walk in disobedience. Deciding who is friends with you will be one of the most important decisions you will make in this life other than accepting Jesus Christ as your Lord and Savior.

Selecting people to be your friends should not be this careless activity but rather a prayerful and thoughtful process. Unlike your acquaintances in the next chapter, your friends will have the permission to lead you down a trajectory where you do not belong, and your friends will have the opportunity to construct your core values and spiritual beliefs.

So, what characteristics should I look for in a friendship? I will take my most extended friendship with my wife Lenora of almost 40 years to offer some practical tools. Friendship is a matter of character and trust. Too often, we choose people to become part of our social circle before examining their character. Do you have similar core values and spiritual beliefs?

What are your expectations as you move people up your social pecking order? Do you want to be able to enjoy their company? Do you expect them to be supportive? How much information are you willing to share with them? Does it matter if they have multiple friends that don't include you?

In this season, many people do not understand why God places certain people in their life. And so, in many cases they abuse and misuse these relationships. If you do not understand the purpose of a thing, you will abuse and misuse it. I believe that there are at least three types of God ordained friendships. I've experienced these three types of friendships in my personal life.

Mentor Friendship

These are God ordained relationships whereby we teach, counsel, disciple, correct, and love unconditionally. We are the ones who pour into other people. Our role in this person's life is hierarchal. We understand as a mentor that there is something that God wants us to pour into someone. Some friendships will be this way. An impartation from the mentor to the mentee must take place. This type of friendship must have mutual respect, loyalty, and a clear understanding of the role of the mentor and the mentee if it's going to work.

Mentee Friendship

That is the person receiving from the mentor. Now let's be clear because I've seen too many Christians mess up this type of relationship, especially in ministry. This person is in a position where you know God has put you into a person's life to get everything out of them related to wisdom, training, and impartation from the mentor. Now I've seen many people, especially in the church, mess up a perfectly good relationship because, after a few training sessions and a few impartation opportunities, the mentee thought they knew more than the mentor. **"Pride goes before destruction, a haughty spirit before a fall." (Proverbs 16:18 NIV)** My father, the late William D. Griffin, was a theologian in his own right. He was my most influential mentor. But even today, I must confess that with all my seminary training I will never know more than my mentor. If you get to where you are and do not have someone to mentor you, you won't go too far. You will never get to a point in your life where you do not need a mentor. You will always need a master teacher. I'm so blessed to have great mentors in my life that I highly respect because they are God-sent. There is safety in the company of many counselors or mentors. In this season, you need people in your social pecking order that will push you, counsel you, and tell you the naked truth with no fluff. You must trust that God sent these people in your life to impart into you. You can't be easily offended by what they say when they mentor you. Be a consistent student who unlearns destructive behaviors and learns new behaviors from your mentors.

Mutual Friendships

This type of friendship is not dependent on mentoring. There are situations where two individuals are aligned spiritually, emotionally, and intellectually. They recognize the relationship is not unilateral or one way. Instead, it flows both ways. One of the biggest frustrations you can have is in a unilateral friendship. By this, we mean that we pour out, and no one pours back into us. Most pastors are guilty of this type of friendship. They are constantly pouring out but don't have anyone to pour back into their lives. We must have a clear understanding that this thing requires mutual investment.

Four Stages in Relationship

Friendship is a complicated thing. There's no rhyme or reason to it; there is no written set of rules. We meet another person; for some people there is an instant connection. We like them for reasons as simple as having the same type of purse or shoes or as complicated as going through life-changing seasons together. From that moment on, that person becomes a part of our lives. Friendships and relationships are important to God because of the tremendous influence over our lives. We often make many decisions in life based on the counsel of friends. Through friendship, we can significantly impact the lives of others. I have a few close friends that I've had since my younger years that I still call today to receive advice or wise counsel. The subjects may range from marriage, ministry, faith, family, or how to manage a complex crisis. And some of my friends are put in my life to be a great support system when I need it. We have a reputation for approaching relationships with an all-or-nothing attitude. Either we invest ourselves whole-heartedly into a relationship or keep the other person at a distance that might qualify them as acquaintances, instead of friends. It's a stereotype, but there's a kernel of truth at its core, like many stereotypes. When we connect with someone new, there's a temptation to share our souls with people to deepen the connection. Sometimes we share personal information too soon. For many of us, doing this has led to a heartache when you discover the person you opened up to can't be trusted. We react by guarding our hearts and not letting new people get close or move up in the pecking order.

I believe an all-or-nothing attitude towards relationships is not a sign of a healthy or mature relationship. If we want to develop meaningful relationships, we must learn how to let people get close, to move up the social pecking order scale. We also must learn how to block toxic or damaging people from our social circle. This point will be discussed in-depth in another chapter. Our tendency is typically to sort people into categories based on whether we trust them. We sort people into levels of trusted and not trusted and interact with them accordingly. Loosening our boundary reign can be a vital tool for this discovery process if we consciously guard ourselves and develop healthier relationships with other people. Therefore, **it is critical to follow God's guidance in establishing friendships.**

Now every Christian is instructed to "be a vessel unto honor, sanctified, and meet for the master's use, and prepared unto every good work...." He is to **"follow righteousness, faith, charity, peace, with them that call on the Lord out of a pure heart." (2 Timothy 2:21-22)**

There must be spiritual discernment when choosing a friendship or relationship. The fundamental meaning of the word discernment is a **decision making process in which a person makes a discovery that can lead to future action.** In this process of **spiritual discernment**, God guides the person through the Holy Spirit to help them arrive at the best decision. Still, they must be willing to accept what the Holy Spirit brings to light about the person during this discovery process.

Many people lack a clear understanding of the different levels of relationships, which involve mutual respect, accountability, specific freedoms, boundaries, commonality, and responsibilities, depending on the relationship scale. The four stages of relationships are (1) **Acquaintance-SHIP**, (2) **Casual Friend-SHIP**, (3) **Close Friend-SHIP**, and (4) **Intimate Friend-SHIP.** To better understand the relationships, we share and the unique roles in our lives, let's take a deeper look at the four stages in relationship.

I want to begin with the bottom scale first.

1st - Acquaintance-SHIP

These are the people we've just met or those who we've known for a while but still interact with at a "shallow" level. At this level, you pretty much treat everyone the same, whether we like/agree with them or not. We don't encourage deep conversations with acquaintances. We nod and smile when they're talking to minimize the risk of conflict, and we answer their questions in a fast, friendly way before making our escape. This scale of friendship is characterized by occasional contact and conversation. Acquaintances are associates in frequent contact with each other, but they don't know each other quite well. They interact only in superficial ways and don't share their lives' emotional or intimate content. There is no shared time you spend together. You may see this person out of obligation but not necessarily desire. Conversations you share are typically formidable but generic, lacking any substance or significant personal connection. Acquaintances are often neighbors, coworkers, or even church members that you share polite interactions, people from school or a gym member that you greet in passing but don't keep in touch with; or even a friend of a friend you see on occasions but don't particularly enjoy their company. An acquaintance is someone you know a little about, but they're at the bottom of your social pecking order scale. You know where they work, how many children they have, what color SUV they drive, but that is the extent of the relationship. The root of acquaintance is the Old French word acointier, meaning "make known."

Being the acquaintance of a person doesn't mean that you will remain at the bottom of the pecking order scale. Still, the other person doesn't know you in a close or intimate way yet. Even people we see frequently can indefinitely stay on the acquaintance trust scale. It would include people we associate with but don't agree with or trust. Trust in any relationship must be earned over time. There are people you force yourself to be cordial to, but you don't necessarily want to be around. Those people could be a family member who dislikes you because of your success, or who argues and shouts whenever you bring something you dislike to their attention, or your friend's emotionally draining mother, or an in-law who imposes their rigid denominational and political views on everyone else. A side note here: just because you attend the same church doesn't mean you know the person. Just because you have the same family name doesn't mean you know the person. Just because you worked together or attended the same college doesn't mean you know the person. You are not who you were five years ago. People tend to assume they know you without developing knowledge of who you are.

2nd - Casual Friend-SHIP

A scale-up from an acquaintance is the casual friend, a scale people might be tempted to skip. We either want people on the friend scale or keep them on the pecking order as acquaintances. The people I think of as casual friends usually must contact me if they want to get together. I enjoy seeing them when we connect, but I don't go out of my way to make that happen. A word to the wise, don't be so quick to put an adjective like very good, best, or BFF to this scale of friendship until the friendship has been proven, tested, and tried. This discovery process takes years to develop. A casual friendship can develop quickly, even during your initial contact and conversation with another person. As you discover common interests, concerns, and respect, you may be given the freedom to ask more personal questions about the other person. As a teenager, I remember this stage in my personal life when my wife Lenora came to the church I grew up in with her aunt.

I hadn't seen her in such a long time, by then we were both teenagers. We exchanged telephone numbers and, over time, became casual friends. But I didn't stay too long at the bottom of the pecking order scale. I moved from acquaintance-SHIP (attending the same church) to casual friend-SHIP developing contact and conversation around more personal topics like goals, opinions, likes, and dislikes. Casual friendships develop when you discover you have common interests, chemistry, and compatibility with another person. You enjoy each other's company. You are on a social scale where you are comfortable sharing personal conversations but do not seem to go out of your way to connect. We usually spend it on the people we're already close to or people we want in our close social circle. We have a limited amount of social energy. However, this limitation holds us back as we pursue deep friendships.

Cultivating casual friendships can be an excellent way to start deepening relationships with people and learning whether you can trust them. It's also a great way to give people a second chance and not fall prey to judging them too quickly. You might find that someone you weren't interested in talking to at first becomes a good friend upon further acquaintance. **Never let other people's opinions about someone force you to move them up or down your pecking order scale until you first get to know that person for yourself.** I've experienced this many times over the years. And what I know to be true is some people are shallow and choose not to think for themselves. They will move you down the pecking order scale without just cause or notification. A cardinal rule helps me not make assumptions or form premature negative conclusions or opinions is this: I never allow people to warn me about people I have not met that would affect my social ranking. So, I advise you always get to know a person for yourself. What if you meet my enemy before you meet my friend?

As your casual friendship develops, you must allow the Holy Spirit to share with you about the other person's behavior, belief system, family history, and character traits. Casual friends share limited emotional data and feelings in careful and watchful ways. Everyone good to you is not good for you. Be honest about what you discover in this stage and acknowledge the facts you observe.

Note: To all the women that are reading this book. I hope this doesn't offend you, but if it does, this statement can save you a lot of pain and disappointment. **Please believe him when a man tells you that he only wants a casual relationship with you. He is simply communicating that he is not ready to commit to you emotionally nor move you up the social pecking order scale**. Being emotionally unavailable is natural when a man doesn't want a commitment or is not emotionally ready to move you up the pecking order scale. He's not going to be there for you emotionally because that would imply, he's into you and the relationship. In my opinion, men can have casual sex with a woman and never get emotionally attached. It's possible to feel a sense of attachment after having sex with someone you weren't that interested in nor have absolutely nothing in common.

The hormone, oxytocin is released into the body during intercourse. This hormone is linked to positive social functioning and is associated with bonding, trust, and loyalty. If we were in church, this would be a good time to say, "Amen!" As a Pastor and Christian counselor, I encourage couples to refrain from sexual activity outside of marriage. If you're having sex (or thinking about having sex) without being married, God wants you to stop. ***"Marriage is honorable in all, and the bed undefiled: but whoremongers and adulterers God will judge."* (Hebrews 13:4)** This verse is not designed to bring judgment nor condemnation, but this is a warning against premarital sex. This is what I call a proceed with caution verse.

God is not against having sexual relations. He designed it to be so intense, exciting, memorable, and fulfilling that He desires us to share the sexual side of the relationship with one person: our spouse. So, if you haven't had sex yet, whether you are single, divorced, or never been married—keep waiting, you'll be glad you did! If you've already had sex, admit it to God, He already knows. He wants to forgive you, give you strength to wait with the help of the Holy

Spirit, and give you a fresh new start. You can start over today—right now while you're reading this book. Talk to God. He's waiting and willing to forgive. Why? Because He loves you! It doesn't mean that the person you're with can't move up in your pecking order scale, but you are still getting to know the other person, so wait while you're going through this discovery process. Wait until all the facts are in; keep asking questions about the other person while you're waiting for answers—God has all the answers! I'm so glad I waited when it came to this casual friendship scale, and you will be happy you did too.

3rd - Close Friend-SHIP
Close friendships are a scale above casual friendship. You have bonded over shared interests, goals, struggles, and invested effort and time with one another. You seek advice from your close friends, celebrate successes with them; you feel comfortable in their presence when you're with them. You probably spend the most time with these friends. A close friendship involves **Fellow-SHIP. Koinonia** is a transliterated form of the Greek word which refers to concepts such as communion, or fellowship, joint participation, the share which one has in anything. Its origin is in the Greek word koinonia, which means partner, sharer, and close companion. Fellowship involves the oneness of the soul (the mind, will, and emotions). It is a shared community that involves deep, close-knit

participation among its people. Many people never really enter this kind of relationship because they're afraid of being hurt or don't truly understand the revelation of this relationship. Although some are tempted to substitute the word fellowship for koinonia, it is more profound. Fellowship is a more surface-level, friendly relationship, while koinonia is full, intimate unity. Koinonia is an essential component in the New Testament church. The apostles became filled with the Holy Spirit in the book of Acts. They helped establish the first communities of new believers who shared in the spirit and all aspects of life together. From meals and homes to money without the fear of rejection. We can have many acquaintances and casual friendships with both believers and non-believers. However, true fellowship (koinonia) requires that both persons share the same relationship responsibilities and life goals to achieve this level of intimacy.

4th - Intimate Friend-SHIP

The fourth most profound level of friendship in my ministry experience is commitment. The commitment to **generously invest in one another's lives to help each other mature in Godly character. "As iron sharpens iron, so a friend sharpens a friend." Proverbs 27:17 (NLT)** Most people never reach this level of intimacy in a relationship. We sometimes see people God has purposely put in our lives to sharpen us as a threat to our development. I believe honesty, humility, accountability, mutual respect, and discretion are requirements of an intimate friendship. You should comfort one another through trials and sorrows and pray diligently for one another.

I discovered in my marriage that friends should have the freedom to **correct each other and point out each other's blind spots without becoming defensive.** It takes time, experience, and maturity. Don't simply point out only character deficiencies; discern their intention and suggest solutions. Search the scriptures for keys to solutions, and be a faithful, loyal friend, which is a rare trait nowadays as you encourage one another to pursue spiritual maturity. This level of friendship can cure loneliness. Every person needs someone at this scale of the pecking order who will genuinely invest in your health, happiness, and success. If you've moved this person up your pecking order scale, this is the person you share all your achievements with and who has seen you at your worst and helped you through your dysfunction, and lowest points. Your connection with this person runs deeper than with anyone else. You understand each other, support each other, and you work to make each other better (most of the time). Let's keep it one hundred. You can go months without seeing each other, and yet the moment you do it's as if no time has passed. This relationship stands on mutual respect, honesty, loyalty, commitment, boundaries, and shared investments, not just some shallow title.

I don't want to close this chapter without giving you a challenge. Take a moment to reflect on the people in your life, specifically anyone you consider to be a friend. Now compare the relationships you share within each of these stages. You will recognize that these friendships play a different role in your life. While some of these roles are more significant than others, I believe each type of friendship fulfills a critical social need. You need different kinds of friendships in your life, not just your besties in your life, whether you realize it or not.

While each friendship is unique, their formation most likely followed a similar trajectory. Whether your friendship was instant or developed slowly over time, a few actions and qualities were present to take that friendship to the next pecking order. Creating a lasting friendship takes time, commitment, work, and a combination of emotional and physical building blocks. But not every friendship will grow and develop into a can't-live-without-you, lifelong relationship. But every friendship has the potential to bring value and happiness to your life, right where they are in the pecking order scale. **"Friendship marks a life even more deeply than love. Love risks degenerating into** obsession; friendship is never anything but sharing." -Elie Wiesel

obsession; friendship is never anything but sharing." -Elie Wiesel

CHAPTER 5

Unpacking the Relationship Gift

Let's examine the relationship and unwrap this gift. In chapter four, I introduced you to the four stages in relationships (1) Acquaintance-SHIP, (2) Casual Friend-SHIP, (3) Close Friend-SHIP, and (4) Intimate Friend-SHIP. As you move up the social pecking order scale, you will experience a range of emotions that you must prepare for if the relationship is to survive.

Every relationship starts on a **superficial** or **shallow level**; you don't really know the person, and they really don't know you. You meet them, through Facebook, social gatherings, or through a family member. You say hi and you move on—unless one of you chooses to take it to the next level. A **superficial person** is all about the surface of appearances. It is best not to expect much from this kind of person without much substance. **Superficial people** care about one person only, and that's themselves.

Many of our daily interactions with people occur on this level in the workplace, marketplace, community, and even the church where we worship every Sunday. But if you don't go to the next level in any relationship and choose to stay superficial with all people, you will be a miserable, isolated, and lonely person. I see so many people on this level living a life of regret. That is not what God intends. Remember Genesis 2:18? It was not good then, and it's not good now for us to be alone!

That is what I called in a previous chapter, the discovery process. Gathering information is when you ask people questions to collect data about them, like where they are from, what they do, where they attend church, where they attended school, their marital status, etc. Most of us have many relationships at this level—that is, Acquaintance-SHIP. As you learn more about someone and sense a connection, you are in the process of progressing to the next pecking order.

Anytime you move up the pecking order scale, you will experience **vulnerability**. Vulnerability is exposure to the possibility of being attacked or harmed, either emotionally or physically, in some cases. The original use of the **term vulnerability was to describe "being able to be wounded or hurt."**

In the Bible, when a city's walls were strong and fortified, there was no fear of the enemy getting through. But when any part of the wall (their outward protection) became "vulnerable," the city's residents were likely to suffer harm. In an everyday relationship, vulnerability is the willingness to be transparent and open yourself up to another person at the risk of being wounded or hurt. **You cannot experience growth in any relationship unless there is vulnerability.**

It has seemingly become cool to talk about our problems. I want to expound on this subject a little more. It's essential to see the difference between being transparent and being vulnerable. For whatever reason, our culture now places a high value on transparency.

The airing of our dirty laundry on social media is often mistaken for vulnerability. A window is transparent. That which is transparent allows objects to be seen clearly through it. We can see a tree outside, but guess what? We can't fully experience the tree. We're able to make several observations about it, but we can't touch it, hear it, smell it, or taste it.

Being vulnerable involves risk. When you are vulnerable with someone, you allow that person to experience you and know you. Being vulnerable is taking the chance to share something about yourself that is deeper than just how your day was! It's more about something at your core that's key to who you are or how you feel about something.

At this level, in the pecking order, you aren't just offering facts to another person; you are choosing to share how you feel about something or someone. Being vulnerable requires constant risk because you are putting something about yourself "out there" without guarantee of receiving something in return. I experience this often as I preach God's Word to His people. I don't always know how people will receive the message, but I deliver God's Word anyway.

It's our responsibility as Christians to be vulnerable with each other and to pursue deep relationships in which we truly get to know each other. Apostle James said it best, **"Confess your faults one to another, and pray one for another, that you may be healed." (James 5:16)** It is a deliberate choice we make, and the more we choose it, the more we know or gain intimate knowledge about how vulnerability looks and feels.

This level is where the flow of relationships splits into one of two outcomes when you choose to be transparent and vulnerable, open up, let down your "protective walls," to risk with someone—you will either feel accepted or rejected.

Lets' talk about rejection! **Rejection occurs when someone deliberately excludes a social relationship or social interaction**. That includes interpersonal rejection, romantic rejection, and family estrangement. In the pecking order, a person can be rejected by an individual or an entire group of people. Jesus experienced rejection by both individuals and religious groups of people. I've also experienced rejection by individuals and religious groups of people or what I call "church folks."

Rejection can cause us to feel various emotions, ranging from confusion, to sadness, to rage. Often, people don't precisely understand the reason for rejection, which can lead to a downward spiral of negative introspection and an overall sense of not feeling "good enough." What makes us feel rejected when we share something personal with another person? We may get laughed at, criticized, ignored, privately or publicly embarrassed, and so on. The natural response when we experience rejection is to:

Shut Down Emotionally.

Much like what you'd expect from a stone if you talked to it! Married couples, single women, men, and even Christians, if they are honest, have all experienced emotional shutdown. People shut down emotionally as a self-defense or self-preservation mechanism. It's after they can no longer cope with the consistent rejection and abuse, that they are enduring they shut down and go into survivor mode. We don't like this feeling of rejection, so we decide then and there that we will never go there again emotionally with that person (or people group). That's why I encourage people in my counseling sessions who've been hurt in a previous relationship to get healed and made whole before they move on to another relationship because hurt people hurt people. If we choose this response repeatedly, we will become: **Impenetrable.**

Impenetrable comes from the Latin word impenetrabilis, meaning "not to put or get into, enter into." Impenetrable means inaccessible to knowledge. This word describes someone impossible to get through. They're like a brick wall, or it isn't easy to read their emotions. Something impenetrable won't let you in. We tend to build walls against people when they've hurt us instead of us confessing our faults to one another. But if we practice this too much and with too many people, guess what? We'll remain: **Superficial.**

When we remain superficial with others, we remain in a state of loneliness and isolation. That is not God's will; He made us for relationship. Unfortunately, people who decide (and it is a choice that people make over and over) to live like this tend to live a bitter, lonely, sad existence. And, if this continues over an extensive period, they will usually develop a cold, callous heart.

Hebrews 3:13 (NIV) says, "Encourage one another daily, as long as it is called "Today," so that none of you may be hardened by sin's deceitfulness." Listen, readers! We need each other! We need relationships because we need encouragement from each other to keep us from becoming insensitive, unsympathetic, and calloused by sin. Let's be honest you can find encouragement on any scale of the pecking order if you allow it.

Acceptance means to be in the embrace of what is without resistance. Acceptance of an offer is the act of saying yes to it or agreeing to it. Acceptance is the other possible outcome of vulnerability. When we share something personal and it is received with attentive listening, sincere questions, good eye contact, and shared emotions, we feel safe to offer more data about our lives. Growing up with a severe speech impediment shaped me into this shy, quiet introvert who struggled with good communication skills. I now try to practice these principles: attentive listening, sincere questions, good eye contact, and sharing emotions with my wife and those I serve. My wife, Lenora, has taught me how to grow in areas; I've learned so much from her. Taking a risk will pay off by bringing you into a more intimate relationship with another person. When we feel accepted, this causes us to offer and share more personal information. That is what is known as **Self-Disclosure.**

Self-Disclosure is a process of communication by which one person reveals or discloses information about themselves to another such as your thoughts, feelings, fears, goals, failures, preferences, and experiences. It's a meaningful way to strengthen relationships and build trust no matter what scale you're on in the pecking order.

When we share with more substance, depth, and meaning; our hopes, our fears, our desires, we reveal our true selves to others. During this process, we often make confessions like, "I feel, I think, I am." And this leaves us feeling more known and understood by the person in a relationship with us. Isn't this what we all long for, no matter what scale you're on?

Known and Understood

I've learned in my years in counseling many people across the country, both saved and unsaved; the importance of sensing that another can pinpoint their thoughts and feelings. And on the contrary, how upset they can be when they don't feel understood. In such moments, they experience a break in the relationship, and with that, feelings of uneasiness, awkwardness, aloneness, and irritation become our reality.

Now we're back to the root, the underlying cause of this entire process! We are made in God's image, and He speaks very specifically about the significance of knowing Him. It stands to reason that we, as humans made in His image, also place a high value on being known.

Agape Love

As we feel known and understood by another, we experience what the Bible calls Agape Love. This ancient Greek word, agape, is a Greco-Christian term referring to the highest form of love, and the love of God for man and man for God. This is a love with no strings attached. It's the love that can love enemies. It's stronger than phileo love, which is affectionate and friendly. Eros, romantic or sexual love, can't keep a relationship whole on its own, either. Agape is the only love that loves and expresses itself regardless of the response of its object. It's a love that doesn't say, "I love you if," but one that says, "I love you, period." Agape love is not based on anything we do or don't do—it's unconditional. Let me say unconditional love is impossible without the power of the Holy Spirit. When you have a relationship with God, His Spirit lives in you, enabling you to love someone in a "supernatural" way. Without Him, in and of ourselves, we can't love unconditionally. Often, we must choose to love the people in our lives by faith based on who God is and what He says, not based on how we feel. This principle should occur no matter where people are on our social pecking order scale. Many relationships would still grow and be together if we didn't base the relationship on just a "best friend" or "closest friend" label instead of Agape love. That is the kind of love I want to experience in my relationships. As we experience this kind of love, we set others up for intimate disclosure. This disclosure happens when others become transparent and open up about themselves.

Many couples who have been married for years sometimes struggle in this area. They can display to family members, church members, and even their Facebook followers that they are best friends. We see them out in public eating together, at social gatherings showing public affection towards one another, at church worship, and even doing ministry together. But behind closed doors, they cannot and in some cases, choose not to disclose information about their inner thoughts, likes and dislikes, preferences, dreams, and goals. That takes a lot of work that many people are unwilling to put in. How can you move up the pecking order in any relationship if you're reluctant to disclose intimate things about yourself? My wife recently asked me a question, "Darryl, can we talk about anything?" My reply was, "We should be able to." Then we proceeded after a few minutes of hesitation with a very intimate and needed conversation. I know men we are guilty of holding back sometimes very intimate details about who we talk to, where we've been, and what we are presently doing. Trust me, I can relate, but if you want a relationship of transparency and trust, you must become vulnerable with each other. My wife and I are different but compatible; we see God maturing and changing us as we continue to learn from each other in those differences. **Proverbs 27:17 (NIV) says, "As iron sharpens iron, so one person sharpens another."** This verse has taken on significant meaning for us in over 33 years of marriage.

My wife and I love each other enough to speak into each other's lives, even if what we have to say is hard to hear. So many times, especially in ministry, we are so quick to speak into the lives of others without mastering and maturing in areas ourselves. But that's what living by faith looks like, doesn't it? That's what agape love is about: "I love you, period. Despite the differences and the things about you that drive me crazy."

Vulnerability is a two-way street. Others see how messed up and broken we are, so they feel more accessible and more able to risk sharing things about themselves. Vulnerability encourages vulnerability. (2 Corinthians 6:11-13) One of the results is a lack of judgment. "Here I am—the good, the bad, and the ugly, and I am in no place to judge you for what's going on in your life."

Accepted vulnerability means moving toward each other without the fear of running the other way. That takes time and effort and is an emotional risk because not everyone is safe or healthy or knows how to do this. But as we take the risk and our vulnerability is well—received, we experience trust and safety in a way that allows us to see a glimpse of God in the other person. I promise that's a cool thing, and it's worth it. As others feel known and understood, they also experience agape love. This leads to more self-disclosure, thus creating a cycle of healthy and functional relationships that are deep, meaningful, and loving. That is how we unpack this relationship gift. Now you are ready to move up the pecking order after you've unpacked.

The Traitor's Kiss
How to Overcome the Pain of Betrayal

A traitor is one who betrays another's trust or is false to an obligation or duty. Perhaps one of the most infamous was Judas Iscariot, who betrayed Jesus for thirty pieces of silver from the chief priests. One of Jesus' most trusted disciples, Judas, became the poster child for betrayal and spineless loyalty. Judas made it all the way up the social pecking order scale. He was hand-picked by Jesus to become part of his intimate social circle.

How would you feel if someone called you a Judas? Would you instantly assume you were considered a traitor or disloyal? If so, you would not be alone in that assumption. Merriam-Webster and many other dictionaries give the meaning of Judas as a traitor, especially one who betrays under the guise of friendship.

He even identified Jesus to the Roman soldiers with the kiss of death. Matthew also includes the kiss of Judas in the arrest sequence; however, Luke depicts Jesus questioning Judas: **"Judas, are you using the kiss of friendship to hand over the Son of Man to his enemies?" (Luke 22:48 ERV)** Unlike most of us in relationships, Jesus expected Judas to betray him and knew it would happen. **"And he answered and said, He that dippeth his hand with me in the dish, the same shall betray me." (Matthew 26:23)**

What is so significant about a kiss? Kissing in the ancient world was seen as an act of greeting, intimacy, and affection. The kiss could be on the cheek or the mouth. The value of a kiss is so significant because in relationships, it shows passion, intimacy, desire, and how much you admire and adore a person. It is essential in healthy marriages. I believe married couples should continue passionate kissing and physical affection throughout their marriage. Women use kissing and physical touching to bond with their spouse and they expect soft kisses and physical touching throughout the day. I even kiss my teenage son, Davien. I've been kissing him since he was a baby because I wanted him to feel a special connection to me and experience what it was like to be touched physically by his father in a nonsexual way. For umpteen years, my son has known what it's like to receive unconditional love and an appropriate touch from his father.

Judas' kiss was a traitorous action disguised as a show of loyalty and public behavior. Betrayals are the most painful aspect of long-term relationships and the most difficult to overcome because you can't prepare for them. I'm almost 60 years young; I've been serving in ministry for over 30 years. When you are so in love with the Bride of Christ, you aren't necessarily expecting to be blindsided by betrayal.

But why are we surprised? How many times did God show us that betrayal is part of our story? David was hunted like an animal by the man who had mentored and loved him; this man was part of David's inner social circle. **Betrayal is part of our story.** It's the dark catalyst for the entire story of God's redemption that unfolds throughout the pages from Genesis to Revelation. It's cruel; it injures, cuts deep, breaks relationships, tears down love, and seems to be constantly lurking around. It should be no surprise to us that betrayal lurks in churches too. If God's people betray God, why would we not betray each other? I've known many of my pastor friends who have experienced different kinds of betrayals, each one with an extra wound to their souls. Some have been able to restore relationships while others have moved on to other ministry positions. Yet others have left ministry altogether because the wounds were too severe. Their souls were too crushed, and their families were broken with grief. I still have some painful scars on my life and family as a reminder of betrayals. The Lord taught me something many years ago while serving in ministry. Scars are simply reminders that wounds and injuries you received by serving Christ's Bride are entirely healed. Remaining is a scar, but you can no longer feel the excruciating pain that's associated with that experience. I've experienced betrayal from family members, preachers, church members, and even those part of my intimate social circle. The pain was too real, but it became part of my story. I remember preaching in a revival one night, and the last night of the revival, I noticed that my wife Lenora was upset. When I questioned her, she said the Pastor was unwilling to give me the offering he received in our name. I went into the Pastor's office to receive my revival offering. The Pastor then said to me: "I just lied to the people to get more money." My wife and I looked at each other with disappointment, and I asked this Pastor, "Why would you lie to God's people just for money." The pain and hurt came from several blows: the sting of the lie, the deep injury of betrayal, the awful feeling that my wife and I had been fooled, the realization that I couldn't trust people in ministry I had relied on, and the disappointing emotional wound my wife and I was left with by someone high up in our social pecking order. I remember him being very arrogant and sarcastic. He reached in an envelope full of cash and pulled out a $100 bill and threw it on his office desk, and said, "Take that." I gave the $100 bill back to him and any other monies we had received from him that week during the revival. We left wounded and bleeding, but I told him God would provide. We were very young in our faith, innocent and naive in ministry. This Pastor knew he was doing wrong; he should have been a mentor and father figure to us, but instead, he allowed his greed—his excessive love for money to cause him to commit financial infidelity. He cared more about money than our relationship. Like Judas, he sold us out for money. That was just one example of many that I've experienced. I'm now able to share my story with people as a testimony of faith and victory. Scars are a natural part of the healing process that doesn't go away after some prophet lays hands on you. But in time, most scars will gradually fade, although they never completely disappear. Let me keep it one hundred with you. We will carry these scars of betrayal with us into other churches, ministries, and even other relationships. In every case, betrayal will leave scars, whether large or small.

David said something that ministered to my soul in Psalm 55:12-14 (MSG).

"This isn't the neighborhood bully mocking me—I could take that. That isn't a foreign devil spitting invective—I could tune that out. It's you! We grew up together! You! My best friend! Those long hours of leisure as we walked arm in arm, God a third party to our conversation."

I believe you need to understand what these emotions are and why you are experiencing them before dealing with and overcoming the pain of betrayal. Betrayal involves several stages: Shock, disappointment, distrust, denial, anger, and acceptance.

Judas betrayed Jesus, someone in his intimate social circle. And Judas betrayed Him with public affection—a kiss. Betrayal can be caused by many things (including fear, power, jealousy, and greed) and by anyone in your social pecking order. These reasons can push people, even as close as family members or members in Christ's Body, to act against you for their reasons, even if it means causing you pain. Does the pain of betrayal ever go away? I know many of you want to know. How can I overcome this overwhelming level of disappointment?

There are actions that you can take to heal yourself. Every hurt has its own story, and so does every healing. But I can say this from personal experience: You can heal yourself when you've filled the hole left behind by a betrayal. And you can help heal the other person no matter where they are on your social pecking order when you sincerely drop the need for vengeance. Of course, I felt like getting revenge. I knew a lot of negative things about the character of that Pastor. But it would be best if you learned to "Let go" after betrayal.

Being able to forgive and let go of past hurts in this season is a critical weapon against the enemy of our soul. Being able to forgive and release the betrayal is a way to keep yourself healthy emotionally, spiritually, and even physically. Forgiving and letting go may be one of the most important ways to keep any relationship healthy, including your relationship with God. Now don't misread this chapter. Some transgressions are so harmful and toxic that those relationships can't survive. But forgiveness and releasing your betrayer can still play a role. Here are a few tips that my wife Lenora and I had to apply:

- Be open & receptive to forgiveness.
- Make a conscious decision to forgive and release the other person. Remember, forgiving and releasing doesn't mean you approve of the other person's hurtful behavior.
- Don't seek revenge or retribution; let God fight your battles. Trying to get even will only extend the pain and get you in trouble with God.
- Accept that you may never know the real reason for the betrayal. Don't beat yourself up trying to figure out why.
- Be patient with yourself, don't rush the process. Being able to forgive the other person takes time.

Please know that just because you forgave and released the other person doesn't mean you must keep them in your intimate social circle. There are times when you need to adjust and move people down your social pecking order. After betrayal has caught you by surprise and knocked the wind out of you once, you brace yourself for another blow. I admit after that experience, I approach relationships with caution of trust. I'm still in love with Jesus and His Bride the church, but the betrayal left a permanent scar on me. I'm afraid I don't want to get hurt all over again. So, I pursue relationships and friendships with great caution.

During Communion and Easter Services, we've heard these words a thousand times—**"On the night he was betrayed."**

We've read those words. We've heard those words. Many of us have spoken those words over the communion table. I've even shared those words with my congregation in a sermon. But for the first time, those words were screaming at me, like a hungry baby crying out for a bottle to soothe its hunger pain. Jesus, God in the flesh, the Word incarnate, suffered betrayal at the hands of one of His closest friends—one who was supposed to support Him, stand up for Him, love Him unconditionally; sold Him out for profit. Jesus was stricken with grief and emotional pain.

His own mother watched in despair as He was tortured and executed. And Judas, the betrayer, was so overcome with grief that he took his own life. Jesus' other friends, many of whom were part of His intimate inner social circle, abandoned Him as well and betrayed Him further, denying even knowing Him. That was more than just a sting in the relationship; it deeply cut our Lord and Savior like a sword to the soul.

"On the night he was betrayed…." I want this to resonate in your spirit. **Jesus took the bread, "and when he had given thanks, he broke it and said, "This is my body, broken for you; do this in remembrance of me." (1 Cor. 11:23-29 NIV)** On the night He was betrayed, Jesus did something for me. And He gave me a command to do something for Him. And so, therefore I keep serving His Bride and breaking bread with His Bride and loving His Bride unconditionally. And every time I think about my experiences and remember my sting of hurt and betrayal, I remember that my Lord and Savior felt the sting infinitely more than I ever will because of what He did for me on the night He was betrayed.

That is my story! I keep serving in ministry; I keep praying for His people. I keep forgiving and releasing those who have wounded me. I keep asking God to heal me, stop the internal bleeding of my heart, and help me keep loving the Bride of Christ unconditionally.

CHAPTER 7

Relationship Pitfalls

Hopefully, after reading a few chapters about friendships and the social pecking order scale, it's been encouraging and helpful to you both spiritually and practically. Some of the deep pitfalls you encounter on the rocky road of intimate love can cause a blowout. Careful driving with both eyes on the road will help you avoid the numerous hazards that can wreck your precious bond. Relationships need attention and care like a car needs gas, a tune-up, and an oil change every 3,000 miles. While writing this book, I thought about the word pillar. If someone describes you as a pillar of strength, they're saying you're reliable and supportive in the relationship. Much like a pillar or column of a building that helps hold the structure up. When I was thinking of a word opposite a pillar, I came up with pitfall. **A pitfall is a concealed hole in the ground that serves as a hidden or unsuspected trap, a pit prepared for**

people. Danger and difficulty are adjectives to describe the word pitfall. When I think of the word pitfall, I envision someone being chased through thick woods. Suddenly, out of nowhere, they fall into a hidden pit, becoming captive to the chaser.

I firmly believe in this season we have an enemy (Satan) pursuing us. Satan doesn't want church members, family members, and in-laws to have God-honoring and healthy relationships. So, he sets up pitfalls—dangerous and all too common traps that can ruin or severely damage relationships if we don't recognize them before we fall into them!

Pitfall No. 1 - Manipulation

From a Christian counselor's viewpoint, manipulation is a type of social influence that aims to change the behavior or perception of others through indirect, deceptive, or secretive underhanded tactics. These methods could be considered exploitive and devious by advancing the manipulator's interests, often at another person's expense. We all want to get our needs met, but manipulators use underhanded methods. Manipulation may seem friendly or flattering as if the person has your deepest concern in mind. Still, it's to achieve an ulterior motive.

Be aware! Manipulative people twist your thoughts, actions, feelings, and desires into something that better suits how they see the world. They mold you into something that serves their purposes. Manipulation and control are signs of insecurity, an ugly vice used to belittle others and fix outcomes. Furthermore, it makes others in the relationship feel unvalued.

Now don't get offended; I'm only sharing with my readers my experience of decades of being in ministry. And by the way, I support women serving in ministry. My wife has been serving in ministry with me for over 25 years.

In the same way that many males have a sports gene I think many women have a manipulation gene! It just seems like women are innately good at manipulation—especially guilt manipulation. Sadly, our first experience of this tends to come from our mothers. You could say it's hereditary: Sin was passed down to us in our DNA, and we'll struggle with it until we see Jesus face to face!

Often manipulation is most noticeable in the tone we use. Maybe you've heard statements like this: "Well, I guess I'll just go to the mall by myself even though I am tired and could have an accident on the way. But don't worry about me, I'll be alright." It's also possible to be passive—aggressive in nonverbal communication. For example, your college roommate's dirty dishes have piled up again, and you're fed up with it, but you don't say anything. Instead, you just pile them all up on their desk.

Men manipulate too, but in my experience, women are just natural at saying things in relationships to get what they want. I believe they are better at it than men. But this is a very dangerous trait to have in a friendship on any social pecking order scale, and you are the only one who can control it! First and foremost, you need to watch your tone and choice of words intentionally. A good rule of thumb is simply to say what you mean and mean what you say. Please don't force people to read between the lines to devise and exploit them into giving you what you want.

I've learned to say to people in my life: "Listen! I don't respond well to manipulation or guilt trips." Some people are just so masterful at manipulation that it can feel like they are just throwing one "guilt trip" after another at you! You can emotionally put your hand up and refuse to be hit by them! But when it comes to manipulation, don't let others get away with it either. People in my life soon realize that they won't get very far with me using that tactic. And hopefully, it doesn't stay a part of our relationship.

Many people must unlearn this practice since it's so entrenched in many of our relationships, usually starting with our experiences at home.

Being involved in a godly, healthy, loving relationship is one of the ways to unlearn manipulation, so it can reveal the unhealthy wiring you didn't know existed. That is another reason why it's crucial to have friends in our lives who can speak the truth in love!

Pitfall No. 2 - Expectations

I read a quote somewhere that said, **"Expectations are delayed resentments."** I used to think that expectations would get you in trouble in your friendships. So, I looked up the definition of expectation: "a confident belief or strong hope that a particular event will happen." The synonyms for it are hope, anticipation, belief, prospect, probability. These all sound like nice words!

I don't see why it would be wrong to have hope, belief, or anticipation in friendships. As a matter of fact, I think it's impossible not to have them. There must be a degree of expectation necessary for a healthy friendship. With that in mind, I obviously have to disagree with my former thinking that expectations will get you in trouble in your friendships.

I think it's more accurate to say that unrealistic or unspoken expectations will lead to resentment and disappointment. We tend to have unspoken expectations: "She should've just known that I couldn't make it to her event!" But having understood and agreed upon expectations will eventually lead to healthy friendships. And this reinforces the importance of effective communication, which is a lifetime lesson in relationships. You must talk these things out! Many people struggle in this area.

Pitfall No. 3 - Jealousy

"Jealousy is cruel as the grave: Song of Solomon 8:6." One thing about jealousy is that it brings harm and insecurity to the jealous person rather than the other person involved. It makes you bitter and insatiable with the good things happening around you. Jealousy will poison any relationship in the pecking order scale, no matter where you are. According to **Proverbs 14:30, "envy rots the bones."** Your friends probably don't mean to be poisonous to your relationship. They would not admit to being jealous of what you have. You don't have to dissolve the relationship. Still, this serious problem will need to be addressed if the connection is healthy at some point in the relationship. Jealousy means fear of being replaced. That will stifle growth and suffocate a relationship quicker than anything in friendships. We all have experienced jealousy in our relationships. You start feeling a wide range of emotions first-hand that someone or something is replacing you. It doesn't matter if you're married, single, in ministry or not. Parents sometimes feel replaced by the spouse of their newly married grown child. Friends sometimes feel replaced by someone else getting too close to their close friend. Even in the church, members can display jealousy towards new members for getting much needed attention from their Pastors.

No matter how silently jealousy creeps into the heart, left untreated, its poison will infect relationships and leave behind broken hearts...Jealousy distorts your perspective, locking all your focus on another person's blessings (marriage, ministry, business, career, family) instead of your own.

Here are some ways to deal with the Spirit of Jealousy no matter where you are in the social pecking order scale:

1. Confess jealousy as sin.
2. Choose gratitude and contentment.
3. Learn to celebrate the other person and their accomplishments.
4. Reject any comparison.

Choose by faith to be grateful and content with the blessings God has provided you.

Jealousy will have you avoiding and gossiping about the very people from whom you should be learning.

Pitfall No. 4 - Gossip

Gossip is a relationship pitfall. It erodes one of the fundamental pillars of any relationship trust and limits how other people share intimate details with you on a different social pecking order scale. Let's get real. Gossip is something that almost everyone has done at some point in their life and one of the reasons for that is that it's easy to gossip without realizing it. For example, you can hear some news about someone else's life. News a friend or family member will find shocking, humorous, or outrageous, and you just can't resist telling them.

Closely related to the manipulation gene is the gossip gene. Once again, in my experience, women tend to be good at this very damaging activity!

I love folk-etymology (the origin of a word and historical development of its meaning.) **The term "gossip" is related to the phrase "to sip."** That is why when someone wants to gossip, they would say—"I have the tea"—"to sip."

Politicians would send assistants to bars to sit and listen to public conversations. The assistants had instructions to sip an alcoholic beverage and listen to conversations; they responded to **the command to "go sip," which allegedly turned into "gossip."** Isn't that hilarious? Even if what you heard was based on something initially true, it might later change through different interpretations. Remember that the next time you want to gossip about someone, it may not be accurate.

You can't "Agape" love someone and choose to gossip about that person no matter where they are on your social pecking order scale. They just don't go together. Here's a paraphrase from the "love chapter" of Apostle Paul's letter to the Corinthians: If you really love someone, you will be loyal to them no matter what the cost. You will always believe in them, think the best of them, and stand your ground in defending them. (1 Corinthians 13:7)

Am I believing (and saying) the best in everyone I talk about? Wow! Are you? Imagine what your friendships would be like; instead of gossiping, you controlled your tongue. Or, if when you heard gossip sneak into a conversation, you said, "Stop! I don't need to hear that. It has nothing to do with me." Where's the best place to start combating gossip? You!

Pitfall No. 5 - Two C's
Comparison & Competition

In relationships, people evaluate their opinions, accomplishments, and abilities by comparing themselves to other people for two main reasons. First, to reduce uncertainty in the areas they're comparing themselves. And second, to learn how to define themselves. They can only define themselves in relation to someone else. I'm convinced that the root cause of comparison is pride. **"Pride goeth before destruction, and an haughty spirit before a fall." (Proverbs 16:18)** Comparison results in an over or under-inflated view of self. In relationships, we use incorrect data to compare ourselves to others. Apostle Paul points this out in **Romans 12:6**

(MSG) "Let's just go ahead and be what we were made to be, without enviously or pridefully comparing ourselves with each other, or trying to be something we aren't...."
Comparison always leads to competition. **Albert Einstein said: "Everybody is a genius. But if you judge a fish by its ability to climb a tree, it will live its whole life believing that it is stupid."**
Stop comparing your career path with others. Stop comparing your ministry with others. Stop comparing your marriage with others. Stop comparing your financial status with others. Stop comparing your family and children with others. Stop comparing your social life and your gifts and talents with others. Please stop! Stop! Stop!
Comparison always leads to competition. Here's the truth: In any relationship, someone, no matter where they are on your social scale, will always be better than you—more intelligent, more talented, more attractive, more popular, and more financially successful. The irony? Someone will always be less intelligent, less talented, less attractive, less popular, and have fewer finances.
Psychologist Leon Festinger did a social comparison study in 1954. He suggested that people have an innate drive to evaluate themselves based on others, whether looks, talents, possessions, and more. There are two types of social comparison:

1. **Upward Social Comparisons** are when we compare ourselves to others on a higher social scale who we think are better than we are. **Have you ever noticed comparing yourself to others on a different social scale?** It makes you feel jealous, insecure, anxious, resentful, and unsupportive of others, leading you to compete with them.

2. **Downward Social Comparisons** are when we compare ourselves to others on a lower social scale who we think aren't as good as we are. Have you ever noticed that comparing yourself to others makes you feel overly confident, proud, or satisfied?—morally superior, arrogant, self-righteous, and sometimes plain old mean & nasty towards others? Many are guilty of this all the time.

I read a quote somewhere that said: **"Don't compare your life to others. There's no comparison or competition between the sun and the moon. They shine when it's their time."**

Pitfall No. 6 - Insecurity

Insecurity can arise when your friend participates in activities and interests without you. However, true friends must have their own identity respected and acknowledged. You and your friend are two independent individuals with different identities who have formed bonds to pursue a common goal. Together, you share mutual interests. Separately, you seek your own. When you get an opportunity, ask your friend: "Together, what does a happy life mean to you, me, and us?"

Sometimes, we feel insecure because we look to other relationships status, material possessions, or money to supply us security. These things and friendships simply aren't created to do so. Often when we look deeper into the lives of those who seem to "have everything," we find abuse, drama, reliance on substances, bitterness, violence, and fundamental discontent. They are just not happy in many of these relationships. It's proof that money and possessions alone do not provide lasting security.

Pitfall No. 7 - Lack of Boundaries

Personal boundaries are important because they set the basic guidelines of how you want to be treated and respected. Boundaries are basic guidelines that people create to establish how others conduct themselves around them. Setting boundaries can ensure that relationships or friendships can be mutually respectful, appropriate, and supportive. Examples of personal boundaries might include:

- "Could you not make comments about my weight?"

- "Please don't invade my personal space."
- "I don't accept phone calls before 8 am or after 10 pm unless it's an emergency."
- "I would prefer you not touch my personal belongings."
- "Would you say goodbye before you hang up?"

Pitfall No. 8 - Money

I wanted to list pitfall number eight last. Money has become a sensitive hot-button issue in many relationships. Money is not the greatest threat to your relationship that everyone believes it to be. Money just makes the most straightforward arguments, guaranteed to put everyone at odds. When it comes down to it, lending money to friends and family rarely works out well in my experience because it changes the dynamic of the relationship. I've seen people—even Christians go months without speaking to each other because of their money. Others have entirely sat on the other side of the church sanctuary or stopped coming to church to avoid some church member asking for their money. It goes from family or peers to a creditor and debtor relationship. That can get uncomfortable when the debt never gets paid back. Believe me! I've been on both ends of the spectrum. Nobody wants that kind of resentment and tension in their close relationships/friendships.

So how do you handle the situation when someone close comes to you and asks you to borrow money? I'm not talking about $10 or $20. I know you're not going to like my counsel. But the best thing to do is to say "no."

But there are things that you can do and say no to that can still be very helpful to someone you love in a challenging financial situation. These can still allow the relationship or friendship to flourish despite your refusal to help with John Doe's $1,000 rent or Mary Jane's $400 car payment. Here are two practical things you can do.

- **Offer to give them the money.** That is a practice that my wife and I have done for years. We never loan out money, but we must agree to bless the other person with the amount needed. That way, there is no expectation of payback and resentment that follows when they don't. Only do this if you can afford to do without the money.

However, I don't think it's a good idea to give people money if you know they have been irresponsible in some way. Bailing someone out rarely works; they need a behavior change. Don't contribute to their stupidity and please don't put yourself in a bad financial position trying to solve their problem. God wants us to be good stewards over the money He has entrusted into our care. First, honor God with your tithes and offerings by supporting your local church. Secondly, pay all your bills that are due. You can't pray to God and ask Him to bless you with $1,000 for rent when you gave your rent money away. That then becomes stupidity on your part.

- **Offer Advice**. If you're a good steward with money and know of an excellent solution to their problem, offer it without digging their debt hole deeper. Show and teach them how to work through their financial situation and come out much better on the other side by planning. That is something that I preach, teach, and live. Every year around fall, I hold financial sessions for five weeks to teach people how to save, invest, tithe, give, sow, retire, and many other economic principles. I love the Chinese proverb that says: **"You give a poor man a fish and you feed him for a day. You teach him to fish, and you give him an occupation that will feed him for a lifetime."**

CHAPTER 8

You Better Recognize

When my teenage son, Davien, was about four or five years old, he unknowingly used the phrase **"You Better Recognize."** My wife and I would laugh hysterically every time he would say, "You Better Recognize." Of course, this comical term became words that he would use around the house on the spur of the moment.

I don't know where my son heard these words, but I knew he didn't have a clue of their meaning. This famous quote, widely known for its affiliation with urban culture, is used to relay the importance of realizing what is happening in real-time. That phrase urges you to process the underlying meaning within the message. "You better recognize" is meant to be a rude awakening; it's a call to perform an assessment.

Early one morning, while still lying in my bed, I heard the Holy Spirit say to me, "You better recognize." I wrote the words on a piece of paper next to my nightstand and got up and said to my wife; this will be a chapter in my next book. I'm contemplating writing a chapter about recognizing the differences between male vs. female friendships. Of course, the woman God gave me encouraged and pushed me to write this chapter to impart these words of wisdom to others.

I've been married to my beautiful wife, Lenora, for over 33 years, and we still have to communicate with each other about the differences between men and women in relationships. That will mean investing your time, effort and emotional energy, and a whole lot of patience. Buckle up because this will be a never-ending relationship lesson you will endure until Jesus returns.

The distinction between male and female is genuine and deeply rooted in human nature and human physiology. What's more, I believe that it's universal from culture to culture and that it finds expression in almost every area of life—no matter where you are in the social pecking order. Whether you are husband or wife, have a mother and son relationship, or work with predominantly men in the marketplace or ministry, you better recognize the differences between men and women in relationships.

In the very first chapter of Genesis, it states, **"God created man in his own image, in the image of God created he him; male and female created he them." (Genesis 1:27)** The implication is clear: the distinction between the sexes is not only fundamental to human nature; it's also uniquely reflective of God's divine order. It presents us with a visible image of the unseen Creator. In some way, we cannot fully grasp it. Our Creator wired men and women differently.

Indeed, the difference between men and women is so significant that they're likely to be from different worlds. And I'm talking not only about appearance or physiology but, more importantly, about their psychological and emotional features as well. Yes, that's true; we react and treat situations in various ways, we often do not coincide at all, and it's natural. It's something we cannot change, so don't waste your anointing and prayers trying to change the makeup of the opposite gender. But we can and must accept, respect, and expect to build harmonious solid relationships despite our differences.

But before we begin considering the most substantial differences between men and women, I'd like to mention that we're going to analyze some "average traits or typical behavior" of men and women. However, there are lots of exceptions nowadays.

So, are you ready to learn and recognize the differences between men and women in relationships? If yes, let's get started!

Being a man myself, I've noticed about my relationships with other men, those men tend to deal with one problem or plan at a time (moving from thought to thought). A woman's thoughts generally flow together. My wife and I have had this conversation often. My son, Davien and I can only deal with one thought or task at a time, while my wife's thoughts generally flow together. She's very good at multitasking. We've had many relationship collisions during our 33 plus years of marriage that needed repairs following the crash. These recurring collisions had nothing to do with our love for one another but our lack of recognizing our differences. STOP! Never drive away from the scene of a crash, even a minor one. Report the collision, make an accurate record, and exchange information. Even if you've dented your relationship, developed deep scratches, or damaged your relationship, you will discover that most relationships are repairable. But the repair costs may vary. Once you find out how your spouse or friend of the opposite gender processes emotions, feelings, and thoughts, you're on your way to a happy and healthy relationship.

Most friendships typically form for the same reasons: shared interest, mutual respect, emotional support, and companionship. However, the type of relationship appears to differ between men and women.

Although the dynamics of male-to-male friendships and female-to-female friendships are more similar than they are different, there remains a difference in how the genders view, engage, and interact in friendships. While one is more casual (male friendships), the other is more intimate and personal (female friendships). Men, unlike women, tend to prefer more activity-based friendships, while women tend to prefer more personable friendships.

Men think that all women are different, and Pastor Darryl, there is no way to understand them. I feel you out there, my brothers! Women think that all men are the same, and Pastor Darryl, there is no way to change them. So, what I've noticed is that men are trying to understand women, and women are trying to change men. As a result, we barely understand each other. It would be better for us to acknowledge and recognize that we can gain helpful knowledge concerning our differences by listening to each other.

What Women Need to Recognize about Men

Friendships between men tend to be more side-to-side such as sports, rather than face-to-face. They are more likely to bond by engaging in shared activities. Men tend to value relationships that include shared activities, are less intimate, and, if you can believe this, transactional. Too often, men create transactional relationships and friendships—"You satisfy my need, I satisfy yours." The notion of transaction comes from the business world, where men do things for each other with the expectation of reciprocation. Happy relationships and marriages are not about 50/50 transactions but a 100 percent interaction. Unlike women, men often do not feel the need to discuss details in their lives with a friend or a need to stay in touch weekly.

Interestingly, men can go extended periods, months or even years, without having contact with a friend, yet still consider the other person a close friend. Although male friendships lack intimacy, they are less emotionally fragile than female friendships. It would help if you recognized that men tend to make friends easier. They do not question the other person's motives or feel pressure to disclose private or intimate information to maintain their friendship as women. At the same time, most men may not share their innermost feelings with close male friends. In my experience, they are more apt to share these feelings with non-threatening female relationships like a wife, sister, mother, or other platonic female friends. Men are more likely to remain friends after a heated argument, whereas most women are not. Men tend to hang out more in a group, "the more, the merrier," while women typically prefer to go out with one good close or intimate friend. I've observed in most cases that men are guided by logic and women by intuition. That's why men have more objective feelings; emotions don't prevent them from adequately perceiving what is going on in their environment. Men usually offer solutions to problems; they want to fix what's broken immediately. When most men have a bad day, they don't want to talk about it in detail, like women do. However, they need someone to notice they're upset, disappointed, or discouraged and support them somehow. Sometimes when faced with an unpredictable crisis, men become non-communitive; they need some me-time to think, cope and process things. But women need to talk about it (actually, sometimes they even ignore all solutions that men offer, venting on and on, and repeating their problem). Men ask themselves, "what to do?" Whereas women ask, "how to do?" or "with whom?" When it comes to emotional responses, here's the difference, men are more consistent—they go through several hormonal changes during their lives: in the womb, throughout adolescence, during puberty, when getting married, or fathering their first child—and as they age, they're very stable and balanced. Men value their achievements, but women value their relationships. That's why for most men, the main thing is work, ministry, and career, while for most women, it's family. Men are very sensitive about their professional failures. To feel completely satisfied with their life, a man must be sure that their career achievements are not less successful than most male counterparts. Women also have a kind of competition, but they put the husband and children on their social pecking order scale. Here's something to point out! Men value way too little about what women say, which often leads to our downfall. This independence and isolation sometimes lead to women feeling rejected in the relationship and emotionally abandoned. And lastly, men's perception—for men, it's 100 percent visual every day all day; for women, it's auditory. The word auditory derives from the Latin word audire, meaning to hear and perceive sounds. A man falls in love through his eyes, a woman through her ears; it is all about recognizing this difference.

Contrary to popular belief, it's men I believe that fall in love at first sight. The attraction for men is by sight: they quickly examine the woman they're interested in and begin to act. That is precisely what I did before I married my wife of almost 34 years. While the paramount importance for men is to feel like a man: respected, acknowledged, admired, and just needed. Men are givers by their nature, and the ideal woman is the one who can happily receive and appreciate him as the head of household. Men are "100 percent" or "nothing" type of guys. What do you mean? A man will only give 100 percent to the woman who has his heart. Contrary to popular belief, it's essential for men to feel loved.

What Men Need to Recognize About Women

For women, the appeal and attraction of any relationship is the relationship itself. Women tend to be more verbally and emotionally expressive than men, and it develops into the need to be listened to and necessarily heard. My mom and wife taught me this valuable lesson. Women are more observant due to their inborn ability to focus on small things and these details are a source of female intuition. Remember that irrefutable women's argument "I have a bad feeling about this person?" When the dust had settled, strange as it may have sounded, she was right in 95 percent of the cases! Without any evidence, without any tangible proof, she was right! Warning men, if you have a praying wife, mother, grandmother, or special woman in your life, they have two powerful weapons in their arsenal. That's the weapon of prayer and the gift of intuition that all women have. The saying 'an elephant never forgets' implies that women have an excellent memory box and are unlikely to **forget** anything. They can remember what color suit you wore to your junior prom. My wife, Lenora, would say, "FUNNY!" I believe a woman has a better memory for small or detailed things—a man keeps in mind the core, essential, the essence.

The first time she meets you, she will analyze each word, gesture, expression, smile, face, nails, eyebrows, shoes, and lots of other stuff—they will see you as a whole picture.

In a close relationship, a woman worries about office work, dirty dishes in the kitchen sink, loads of clothes that need washing, and a stain on the baby's clothes. A man doesn't. Let's keep it real; he doesn't even notice something is wrong. "A mess? I don't see any mess. A hole in the wall, I don't see a hole in the wall, a loud noise outside the house, I didn't hear any noises." So, women, don't be shocked if a man tells you, "Oh, I didn't know we had any problems in the relationship. I thought everything was fine." Women also, in my experience, pay lots of attention to others. They will never miss or ignore someone's tear-stained eyes, trembling lips, worried countenance, or unusual demeanor. Men again may not even see that. I've been guilty of this myself.

Women want empathy, yet most men usually offer solutions. Not surprisingly, female friendships tend to be more dependent on face-to-face contact, are more emotional, share thoughts and feelings, and have more mutual support. Women bond by disclosing secrets, lengthy conversations, and spending quality time together (face-to-face). There are also gender differences in how men and women form and sustain friendships.

Another critical difference we must recognize between male and female friendships is the frequency of personal contact, investment in the relationship, and types of emotional challenges/issues discussed. In contrast, if a woman does not have regular contact with an individual she views as a close friend, she is more likely to assume they have grown apart, are no longer interested in the friendship, and assume the relationship has dissolved.

Strange to say, but despite women's emotionality and men's stability that we've already recognized, women are more flexible and resilient in conflicts. Women tend to listen to various opinions of others, summarize pros and cons, and hesitate a lot in decision making. In contrast, men often burst and argue a lot because of the male ego.

Women's patience is particularly evident when it comes to illness or fatigue. It's a popular theory that men get sicker or at least act sicker when they contract any type of cold (not COVID-19), while women soldier on with school, ministry, work, childcare, household chores, and life. I've seen my wife work 10 to 12 hours in the office, cook dinner, carry bags from Walmart with back pain, broken toe, flu-like symptoms, and even a slight fever. But most men turn a runny nose and four coughs into a struggle for survival.

Lastly, I want to touch on a very sensitive subject, physical intimacy. That is not a subject you hear many people touch on in the church. But I wanted to include this subject in this chapter. A man has almost purely visual sexual stimulation, while a woman wants some romance and emotional intimacy throughout the day. Men are easier to arouse sexually. You can't fast and pray this away, women. Women, however, depend on menstrual cycle, mood, atmosphere, emotional well-being or whatever. By contrast, men are attracted by sight, but a man's appreciation and affection stimulate a woman. Men can start immediately, but women need emotional and mental preparation. Also, women may feel so broken and abused when they're forced or pressured into sexual intimacy (even with a husband). Men usually feel just ok about it. Men want to have sex, but women want to make love.

Although these differences recognized in this chapter do not apply to all men-to-men and women-to-women friendship/relationships, this provides a general idea of how men-to-men friendships differ from women-to-women friendships.

Regardless of the type of friendship you are in, it is vital to identify what you are looking for in a friend or relationship. Identifying what you need and want out of a friendship can assist you with determining if the person you would like to be friends with can provide the type of spiritual, emotional, and physical connection you desire.

How to handle these differences?
Most often, the problems in relationships arise when we don't realize or recognize how different all men and women are.

Our inability to accept and respect these differences may lead to continual disappointment, frustration, irritation, resentment, stress, and as a result, the demise of the relationship. So, the key to moving past your differences is to understand them and fix your relationship. It's not too late! In conjunction with understanding comes compromise in any situation; something in between your views so that no one loses or wins.

I will conclude here. I pray all my readers loved reading this chapter on recognizing the differences between men and women in relationships.

FOR YOUR CONSIDERATION

If this book enlightened you, purchase one for a family member & friend. Also, share your favorable reviews on social media.

Other books by Dr. Darryl O. Griffin:
FAITH DEVELOPED IN THE DARKROOM SERIES

"Faith Developed in the Darkroom"
When Your Life's Journey Takes a Turn You Didn't Plan

"Darkroom Faith Workouts"
30 Day Devotional

To order books or schedule Darryl Griffin for speaking engagements, conferences, seminars, or leadership training write or call:

Dr. Darryl O. Griffin
Darryl O. Griffin Ministries
P.O. Box 1333
Cordova, TN 38088
901-205-6991

www.darrylogriffin.com